Hermógenes H. Oliveira Nascimento

Post-Modern Tourism

Hermógenes H. Oliveira Nascimento

Post-Modern Tourism

Dilemmas and prospects for sustainable management

ScienciaScripts

Imprint
Any brand names and product names mentioned in this book are subject to trademark, brand or patent protection and are trademarks or registered trademarks of their respective holders. The use of brand names, product names, common names, trade names, product descriptions etc. even without a particular marking in this work is in no way to be construed to mean that such names may be regarded as unrestricted in respect of trademark and brand protection legislation and could thus be used by anyone.

Cover image: www.ingimage.com

This book is a translation from the original published under ISBN 978-3-330-76787-4.

Publisher:
Sciencia Scripts
is a trademark of
Dodo Books Indian Ocean Ltd. and OmniScriptum S.R.L publishing group

120 High Road, East Finchley, London, N2 9ED, United Kingdom
Str. Armeneasca 28/1, office 1, Chisinau MD-2012, Republic of Moldova, Europe
Managing Directors: Ieva Konstantinova, Victoria Ursu
info@omniscriptum.com

Printed at: see last page
ISBN: 978-620-8-57523-6

CONTENTS

CHAPTER 1

INTRODUCTION

From the mercantile society of the 15th century to the modern global economy of the 21st century, the forces of production have led to a growth in human potential that would have seemed impossible to imagine five hundred, two hundred, fifty or even ten years ago. Paradoxically, the greater the human potential resulting from the infinite capacity to generate knowledge, the more uncertain the future. It seems that contemporary society is running into red lights that challenge its ability to adjust to increasingly rapid changes.

The multidisciplinary nature of tourism activity is emphasised in academia, and is also proven in practice, as it is seen by the diversity of sectors involved, both governmental and private. Perhaps this is why the concepts and definitions of tourism are so complex, which is why it has been so difficult to come up with a concept that covers all the different aspects.

To begin the discussions in this paper, it is worth mentioning Beni's (2001) conception of tourism, in which he adds economic, technical and holistic dimensions to this definition. Likewise, in everyday life, tourism has occupied various categories, be it economic, social, cultural, a means of environmental protection and/or degradation, among others.

Defining this activity is a complex task, as it is a social practice that has changed in form and meaning throughout history, and each new definition faces the difficulty of conceptualising something that has, admittedly, an unquestionable dynamic (Rodrigues, 2003).

Throughout the 20th century, with the increase in the practice of tourism by society and consequently the awakening to the study of the activity, various other definitions of tourism emerged, including a broadening of its complexity, as can be seen in the definition proposed by anthropologist Jafar Jafari (apud BENI, 1991): "it is the study of man far from his place of residence, of the industry that satisfies his needs, and of the impacts that both he and the industry generate on the physical, economic and cultural environment of the receiving area".

Since the late 1950s, tourism has become an important variable in the world economy. Over the last three decades, tourism has been recognised by several countries as a valuable socio-economic development strategy. In this scenario, tourism has emerged as an important instrument for boosting the services sector, since, according to the World Tourism Organisation (UNWTO), the activity generates annual global revenues of more than US$400 billion. The UNWTO predicts that by 2020, world tourism will reach revenues of around two trillion dollars.

It is thus against this backdrop of the evolution of our society that modern tourism has become an activity of great relevance in the world in quantitative terms, producing a large number of journeys due to the technological advances in means of transport, generating jobs and, in some cases, raising the income level of communities, cities and even countries (ANDRADE, 1992). Although some authors still mention that at the beginning of the development of mass tourism after the Second World War, it had some positive impacts due to the benefits provided by leisure. However, in the course of the text, it will be seen that this massification of tourism has, in fact, only led to a number of negative impacts.

According to Ruschmann (1997), tourism can be an option for the development of communities and people. However, it requires rigorous planning, with the participation of the community involved, if it is to be successful .

The fact is, according to statistics published by the World Tourism Organisation (UNWTO, 2006), approximately 6 to 8% of all jobs generated in the world depend on tourism, and tourism is the segment that directly accounts for 10% of the world's Gross Domestic Product (GDP), i.e. it is the fastest growing activity in the world today (LAGE and MILONE, 2000), second only to the oil industry, and as well as involving social and economic relations, it also involves issues of speculation and environmental conflicts. As a result of these factors, it is necessary to investigate its consequences and impacts on sectors of society.

On the other hand, post-modern tourism is gaining momentum and modelling itself on the principles of sustainability, as it offers experiences of great emotional value, since it offers the possibility of interacting with the environment and the local culture, promoting a break from everyday life (WAINBERG, 1998; URRY, 1999). By reflecting on tourism not only as a form of leisure and self-knowledge, but also as a phenomenon that connects people of different cultural identities, this study elucidates the issue of socio-environmental relations, specifically how post-modern tourism or post-tourism can corroborate its conception for sustainable tourism management.

Nowadays, concerns surrounding environmental issues such as global warming, healthy eating, development with less environmental impact, quality of life, etc. have become increasingly frequent. In short, there are discussions seeking forms of production and consumption that fit in with sustainability. By incorporating these thoughts about man versus the environmental crisis, the proposal to carry out this work was born out of the reflection that involves and blends the issues of sustainability and tourism.

It is clear from this work that new assumptions for the planning and management of tourism need to be put forward to support the new environmental, economic, political and social perspectives of today's world.

It's worth mentioning that the management model for a destination to be sustainable is one that adopts a set of systemic, realisable measures and long-term planning, which extends to all phases of a tourist destination's life cycle and combines its development along economic, socio-cultural and environmental lines.

In this sense, Ignarra (2001) takes this approach further when he says that any tourist destination has its own life cycle, and he emphasises that the stages are: Exploration, Development, Consolidation, Stagnation, Rejuvenation or Decline. In this way, it is believed that in order to maintain a consolidated destination or, if necessary, move into a phase of rejuvenation, it is necessary to constantly improve and reposition the market in order to preserve what already exists and attract new opportunities.

In view of this, it is necessary to bring up the pillars that built the concept of sustainable tourism and that will direct all this work in the way post-modern tourism is structured, because according to the UNWTO, based on the Brundtland Report in 1987, it defines sustainable tourism as that which:

> "[...] meets the needs of current tourists and receiving regions while protecting and fostering opportunities for future tourism. [...] while respecting cultural integrity, essential ecological processes, biological diversity and life-sustaining systems". (UNWTO apud DIAS, R., 2003, p.68).

It is worth emphasising that with this same ideology of the Report, one can outline the scope that guides the foundations of post-tourism. Continuing the development of the work, we realise that sustainable management of the activity, according to Beni (2001), requires tourism planning, as well as a system that is integrated with other local activities and must also be structured around a long-term plan and strategic projects.

As a way of justifying the birth of this work, Castrogiovanni (2003, p.45) can be mentioned, as he argues that:

> Tourism wasn't born out of a theory, but out of spontaneous practices that have shaped themselves, which seems to partly justify the fluent reading that insists on treating tourism empirically and as a devourer of landscapes and

> places. It's time to propose an innovative intervention in tourism know-how [...] through the deconstruction of know-how (MOESCH, 2000). Deconstruction is the most appropriate instrument for breaking down paradigms that are so sedimented and creating readings that force the need for continuous questioning of knowledge and information, transforming them into provisional truths and paths with differentiated options.

In the light of the above, by focussing on the problem, this research initially evaluates the history of mass tourism and its impacts, and then discusses the challenges and prospects of post-modern tourism as a way of contributing to the sustainable management of this activity.

In this way, it can be said that tourism is a concrete possibility for minimising regional disparities (CRUZ, 2000). Tourism is therefore an alternative that can boost regional growth and development.

In line with this, tourism can be considered an alternative form of economic exploitation that is linked to sustainability, since its main resources are nature, the local community and its culture, customs and traditions, which must be preserved. In the case of Brazil, ecotourism stands out as a possible catalyst for the tourism business, since the country has enormous potential, presenting a multitude of areas and regions favourable to its practice in these areas. However, tourism must comply with a series of rules, planning and the involvement of the entire community, the public sector, the private sector, NGOs and tourists themselves, so that it can minimise its impacts and be in line with the principles of sustainability.

The study is based on the assumption that by analysing various authors who advocate a new conception of tourism development, these implications will be better substantiated in order to elucidate some questions, which are: What is the purpose of this post-tourism?; How can this activity be sustainable in its management over time?; What are the bottlenecks that hinder the development of post-modern tourism?; And what are the prospects for this tourism to foster an environmental ethic in society?

CHAPTER 2

MASS TOURISM AND ENVIRONMENTAL IMPACTS

Before capitalism, it wasn't possible to think of people's time as an input that could be accumulated by the owners of capital. The imprisonment of time, although not a recent invention, as it had already been observed by Adam Smith in the 18th century[1] , was only effectively noticed, as we know it today, at the beginning of the 20th century, when the immense gains in productivity in industry and greater effects on the environment allowed the inclusion of workers who produced in factories in markets that they were not part of.

Many destinations around the world suffer from the impacts caused by tourism, especially with regard to environmental issues. The use of natural resources as tourist attractions leaves various traces and traces, which over time become impacts that are often irreversible. And this situation is occurring more and more frequently in localities, with the intense increase in tourism worldwide.

The large-scale global demand for natural resources is only set to increase, as the world's population grows and so do its needs and desires. History proves, therefore, that there are several old and new cases of environmental degradation caused by human beings, most of whom have maintained a disharmonious relationship with nature.
There has been a transformation of man's relationship with nature, with the transition from an interface in which overcoming in the search for simple survival predominates (homo culturalis), to an interface in which the emphasis is on mechanical and

1 Adam Smith mentions the effects of the division of labour on the productivity of manufactures: "The division of labour, so far as it can be introduced, generates in every trade, a proportionate increase of labour power....(...) This great increase in the quantity of work which, in consequence of the division of labour, the same number of persons are able to perform, is due to three distinct circumstances: firstly, to the greater dexterity existing in each workman; secondly, to the saving of that time which it would generally be the custom to lose in passing from one kind of work to another; finally, to the invention of a great number of machines which abbreviate and facilitate labour, by enabling a single person to do the work which would otherwise have to be done by many".

specialised overcoming in the search for intense productivity (homo industrialis), overcoming and altering the limits of the environment's provision of well-being for the individual (BARTHOLO, 1984).

Travel, once socially selective, gained mass appeal with the emergence of the train, car and steamship in the 19th century, and later, in the 20th century, with the reduction in their importance and the invention of the aeroplane. The growth in visits to seaside resorts since the 19th century was due to industrialisation and "pleasure was structured in a society based largely on the industrial classes" (URRY, 1996, p.34).

The tourist industry experienced rapid growth in the first half of the 19th century, and a number of seaside resort towns developed. Brighton in England, for example, grew from 7,000 to 65,000 inhabitants in fifty years, becoming a fashionable place and reinforcing the concept of mass tourism based on seaside resorts. Like Brighton, 48 other English seaside towns experienced population growth and a concentration of specialised and unique services, designed to "provide unusual objects for the tourist's gaze" (URRY, 1996, p.36).

A socio-historical analysis of the relationship between seaside resorts and tourism is a good way to start the discussion on tourism and sustainability. Mass tourism has brought about all the effects of the rapid growth of seaside resorts.

This was felt in the form of an increase in population and the consequences: marginalisation, violence, alcoholism, housing shortages and social segregation. Traditional populations were displaced to other places and businesses linked to the interests of the tourist industry were created, such as amusement parks, concert halls, boarding houses and summer residences for the elite.

Mass tourism is a type of tourism that does not lead to the development of the community, but rather of the few who benefit from it, and is often exclusionary, causing various environmental and cultural impacts. And in communities with weak local political power, it causes social inequality with a low degree of social organisation, privileging specific groups and damaging the localities in question, making it difficult to implement sustainable tourism development models (CARVALHO, 2007).

These first manifestations of the massification of tourism with their contradictions, however, cannot be compared to what happened right after the Second World War, from the 1950s onwards. The period from 1951 to 1960 saw the highest growth rate of any observed by the UNWTO. With access to air travel and the organisation of international routes, luxurious cruise ships, comfortable buses and modern passenger trains, millions of people were able to travel more comfortably and quickly (GOELDNER et. al., 2002). Since then, there has been a huge increase in global tourism arrivals (Table 1).

YEAR	ARRIVAL (Millions)	GROWTH PERCENTAGE
1950	25	
1960	69	176%
1970	166	141%
1980	288	73%
1990	457	59%
2000	687	50%
2010	940	37%
2020	1600*	70%

Illustration 01: Evolution in the number of tourist arrivals in the world. Source: World Tourism Organisation. * UNWTO estimate.

It can be inferred from the above that tourism is a fast-growing sector in terms of the global economy. Since the 1950s, when international travel became accessible to the general public, the number of tourists has been growing at an average rate of 6.8 per cent a year (UNWTO, 2005).

It is also worth noting from the figures presented that the rate of growth accumulated over the decades has decreased, meaning that new routes need to be created to meet more demanding demands, as well as consolidated destinations reinventing themselves with sustainable tourism products. One of the biggest challenges facing the global tourism industry is dealing with the issue of seasonality. From the smallest tourist systems to the world's major regions, everyone has to adapt to a global trend of reduced tourist flows at certain times of the year.

According to estimates by the UNWTO (2006), the number of tourist arrivals in 2005 reached 808 million worldwide. Trends for the future of tourism activity suggest that by 2020, international tourist arrivals will be close to 1.6 billion, equivalent to 20% of the world's population. The organisation expects the global tourism sector to grow at an effective rate of 4.1% by 2020 (UNWTO, 2005).

Therefore, the outlook is for East Asia and the Pacific, as well as South Asia, the Middle East and Africa, to grow by more than 5 per cent a year, in contrast to the world average of 4.1 per cent. On the other hand, in the more consolidated regions, such as Europe and America, growth rates are expected to be lower than the average.

It's clear that Europe will continue to be the region with the largest number of international tourist arrivals (717 million), but while in 1995 the region comprised 60 per cent of all tourist arrivals worldwide, in 2020 this figure will fall to approximately 46 per cent. Europe will be followed by East Asia and the Pacific (397 million), America (282 million), Africa (77 million), the Middle East (69 million) and finally South Asia (19 million).

According to statistics from the Ministry of Tourism (BRASIL, 2005), after three consecutive years of below-average growth (2001-2003), the growth rate in 2004 was 11%, the highest percentage and the only double-digit growth since 1980, when began collecting detailed data on the sector. Also in 2004, revenues from global tourism hit an all-time high, reaching approximately US$ 622.7 billion as a result of 763.2 million international tourist arrivals.

This volume of figures is largely due to the expression of mass or traditional tourism, which refers to tourism that began in the 19th century after the Industrial Revolution and intensified in the following century after the Second World War. The main characteristic of this activity was that it was a phenomenon of the industrialised world that occurred due to the availability of free time, improved quality of life, the development of means of communication, transport and new technologies (BARRETTO, 1995; DANTAS, 1999).

In this direction, as a result of modernity, mass tourism is also changing and becoming popular as a modern human leisure activity; it is the result of social and economic transformations, which only emerged and became a reality in the last century as a result of labour conquests; among other factors, it is in the large tourist metropolises that more and more people are discovering opportunities for tourism trips during their leisure time.

Ruschmann (1997) characterises mass tourism as a large volume of people travelling in groups or individually to the same places, usually at the same times of the year. This type of tourism is considered to be largely responsible for damaging natural spaces, as the excess of tourists leads to the oversizing of equipment related to the superstructure of tourist facilities, which occupy large spaces, damage landscapes and destroy ecosystems. And it can be seen that the tourist culture of these visitors generally shows little or no concern for the preservation of nature or local culture.

Specifically addressing the impacts caused by tourism, Ruschman (1997, p. 34), considers that, "the environmental impacts of tourism refer to the range of changes or sequence of events caused by the process of tourism development in the receiving localities".

According to Coriolano (2006), the environmental impacts of tourism are the result of the process of touristification of landscapes or the process of changing a place in order to make it suitable for tourism, when the pace and volume of resource exploitation cannot be synchronised with the environment's capacity to support this exploitation.

The growing evolution of tourism at a global level driven by socio-economic factors has stimulated the need to provide a range of infrastructures, which in many cases have been designed inappropriately without a prior environmental impact assessment.

Corroborating this fact, Cruz (2001) states that the impacts of tourism on natural environments are associated both with the placement of infrastructures in the territories so that tourism can take place, as well as the movement of people that tourism promotes in the places; accommodation facilities built in non-urbanised areas, as well as other infrastructures associated with them, can represent significant risks of destabilising the ecosystems in which they are located.

Furthermore, the voluminous flow of tourists worldwide has caused social, economic, cultural and environmental impacts, the scale of which has only recently been the subject of concern on the part of society. Measuring the impact of tourism is as difficult as the challenge of defining its sustainability. In fact, due to its heterogeneity, there are difficulties even in defining tourism as an industry or even in conceptualising what tourism and tourists are (LICKORISH & JENKINS, 2000).

Against this backdrop, the UNWTO (2006) notes that mass tourism is still in its initial phase because, unlike elitist tourism, it still retains an important latent or potential demand, depending therefore on the economic situation and particularly on the increase in the purchasing power of the middle-class population, generating a target audience that is eager to travel. However, it is believed that the UNWTO's position on the middle class needs to be addressed, i.e. the best way to conceive mass tourism needs to be diagnosed and acted upon with strategic planning so that destinations don't have their carrying capacity overloaded with demands that are not yet prepared to enjoy tourist landscapes with socio-environmental responsibility. It's worth pointing out that tourism education is one of the alternatives for making the most of travelling.

Conventional tourism has a more negative impact on the tourist destination than alternative tourism. Conventional or mass tourism, according to Fennell (2002), is characterised by the fact that it dominates tourism in a region and contributes very little to local development, since the financial resources don't stay in the region. As a result, the hotel and other facilities are generally produced with external products, there is little demand for regional food and marketing encourages large numbers of people, often marked by seasonal demand, which influences the levels of employment offered in the locality, altering the rhythm of life of the local population and directing actions towards satisfying customer expectations and demands.

The tourism business is based on satisfying visitors' needs and exoticism is one of the appeals used by some destinations to attract them. Many tourists are eager to get in touch with nature. For this reason, an extremely critical factor in tourism is that the more fragile or threatened a particular environment is, the more attractive it becomes for tourism, thereby potentiating its negative impacts. The diagram below shows the most important impacts.

- Creation and deterioration of trails	- Reducing habitat size
-Deterioration of camping sites	- Irregular collection of plant and animal specimens and impacts on vegetation
- Saturation of visitor numbers at some tourist sites	- Soil compaction and erosion with increased trampling by people and horses
- Impacts caused by transport and recreational vehicles	- Increased fishing and reduced fish stocks
- Accumulation of rubbish	- Visual and sound impacts
- Disturbance of routine or impacts on fauna	- Increased risk of fires
- Environmental use conflicts	- Changing the course of rivers and streams
- Physical or biological water pollution	- Damage caused by vessels
- Proliferation of weeds, fungi or exotic species	- Emissions and air pollution

Illustration 02: Negative impacts of the tourist flow on the environment. Source: Adapted from Eagles, McCool and Haynes (2002, p. 33).

From this point of view, it can be seen that poorly planned and managed tourism can have negative effects, symbolising dangers for the region and bringing impacts to the environment of specific types and in specific ways, such as damage to soil and vegetation, pollution to watercourses, loss of life for flora, fauna and wild habitats and an increase in the amount of rubbish in places visited, as well as vandalism to natural ecosystems and other indirect environmental impacts. Writing about the environmental impact of tourism, Cooper et al (2001, p. 186) state that:

> There are no generally accepted models for environmental impact assessment (EIA). In many environmentally sensitive tourist destinations, there are few legislative acts and even fewer bodies with powers to safeguard the environment in relation to tourism development [...].

For Buckley (2003), what predetermines the success of tourism in natural areas is an understanding of the ecosystems where it takes place and a correct assessment of the impacts that can occur there. There are countless sources of impact, including the creation of the infrastructure required for the activity, the adaptation of transport and the installation of accommodation facilities.

Andereck (1994) found that the issue of solid waste production and water pollution seems to be more serious in less developed countries, where there are no more advanced systems and technologies for composting the large quantities of waste produced by the tourist industry, mainly by hotels, transport and catering companies.

The environmental damage that exists in this industry is similar to that which exists in many other economic activities. However, it is the tourism industry that perhaps has the most powerful incentive to keep the environment clean and healthy: maintaining its image in the eyes of the market. As Goeldner, Ritchie & Mcintosh (2002) state, in many places there is a drop in demand when environmental degradation increases, because tourists systematically avoid polluted places. For this reason, the quality of the environment is a factor in the competitiveness of tourism, as Mihalic (2000) states. He lists various marketing and management elements for competitiveness, such as: certification of good practices and the drawing up of codes of conduct, among other efforts.

For this reason, a discussion that may be pertinent from the point of view of tourism sustainability is the inclusion of the ethical dimension that will necessarily permeate its management and commercialisation. One of the proposals for conceptualising sustainable tourism expresses this concern:

> Sustainable tourism involves a more productive and harmonious pursuit of the relationship between the visitor and the host community and the place (and its immediate surroundings), a situation that can be maintained without exhausting resources, misleading the visitor or exploiting the local population (GARROD & FYALL 1998, p.201).

Thus, in order for the tourism sector to be utilised with greater responsibility, profitability and fewer harmful impacts on the environment, it is necessary to identify the environmental impacts associated with the development of tourism activities at an early stage, before nature can feel the presence of human activity in a pernicious and definitive way.

At this point, it is important to note that tourism has undergone a brutal evolution in terms of the flow of travellers, causing numerous positive and negative effects that have already been noted, and which will be explored in depth in this book from a general viewpoint of tourism management.

According to everything listed here, the discussions on mass tourism are important parameters for the tourism expert to think about, analyse and propose measures for the entire production chain that surrounds the activity, as this serves as support for implementing more rational tourism and are trends that have been confirmed in new forms of management that will be presented in the course of the work.

As such, the development of actions, attitudes and practical applications by society, public and private organisations, in projects, research and in various other ways, that enable tourism to interact with protection and preservation measures, with a sustainable approach, has become more important and necessary. The interaction between man and nature must develop in a mutually beneficial relationship, so that it is good for the user and does not have a major impact on resources.

CHAPTER 3

POSTMODERN TOURISM AND ENVIRONMENTAL ETHICS

When post-modern tourism is analysed on a global scale, taking into account the differences that exist between the regions of the planet, it allows us to question the management that has been practised in these destinations, in order to identify which characteristics make them more evident, since they present themselves in an exotic way on the tourist market, and will therefore require researchers to make a careful assessment of this new tourism arrangement. And so we can examine the extent to which the current tourism scene in newer destinations is similar to that of consolidated destinations. And how these new tourism products look in the 21st century.

There have been several efforts, involving governments, international organisations, operators and academics, to standardise tourism. These initiatives seek to conceptualise sustainable tourism, standardise existing legislation, harmonise conflicts and suggest certification methodologies, among others.

The environmental development agenda of the 1960s and 1970s led to much attention being paid to the impacts of tourism in the 1980s and to the emergence and/or development of terminologies to describe various forms of tourism that were considered, in a way, different from those that had emerged before. For example, from mass tourism to green, sustainable or ecotourism (LESLIE, 2012). These are terms that emerge as alternative forms of tourism with an association to sustainability, such as ecological, soft, endemic or low-impact tourism (RUSCHMANN, 2002 apud COSTA, 2013).

Perhaps one of the most important global collective manifestations for the definition of sustainable tourism is the Manila Declaration of the World Tourism Organisation (WTO), adopted in 1980, which emphasises the importance of natural and cultural resources for the development of tourism and the need for their conservation for both the tourism sector and resident communities (THEOBALD, 2002).

The World Conference on Sustainable Tourism held in the Canary Islands, Spain in 1995 resulted in the Lanzarote Charter for Sustainable Tourism, which presents 18 principles of tourism sustainability summarised in four, as Muller points out (apud ANDREU, 2003, p.32). Illustration 03 shows the principles of the Lanzarote Charter, which can be summarised as:

- Protecting and restoring natural resources;
- Quality of life for local communities;
- Satisfying the needs of tourists;
- Respect for local culture.

1. Tourism development based on sustainability criteria. It must be: ecologically sustainable; economically viable; and ethically and socially equitable for local communities.
2. Tourism must contribute to sustainable development and be integrated with all aspects of the environment, respecting fragile areas and promoting the assimilation of impacts, taking into account the limits and capacities of nature.
3. Tourism must consider its effects on the cultural heritage and traditions of local communities.
4. The participation of all players in the development process is essential.
5. Conservation of nature and cultural heritage involves co-operation, planning and management.
6. Tourist satisfaction and the preservation of destinations must always be established with local communities and guided by principles of sustainability.
7. Tourism must be integrated into local economic development.
8. Tourism development must improve the quality of life of local populations.
9. Tourism planning is important.
10. Balancing the benefits and burdens of tourism must be considered.
11. Special priority should be given to environmental and cultural vulnerabilities and already degraded areas.
12. Alternative forms of tourism compatible with sustainable principles should be promoted.
13. Research must be promoted.
14. Environmentally compatible management systems should facilitate sustainable tourism policies.
15. The travel industry should promote sustainable development, exchange of experiences, etc.
16. Particular attention should be paid to transport and the use of non-renewable energies.
17. Codes of conduct must be established for the main players.

18. All the necessary measures must be implemented to promote awareness of sustainable tourism among everyone involved in tourism.

Illustration 03: Charter for Sustainable Tourism.
Source: Lesley France. The Earthscan Reader in Sustainable Tourism.

Attempts to define what sustainable tourism is are criticised for the danger, according to some scholars, of defining something of an extremely complex nature, whose implications and relationships cannot be reduced to the simplicity of a concept outlined in one or two paragraphs (SWARBROOKE, 2000).

What common ground can be found regarding the sustainability of tourism? In order to arrive at an answer, it is first necessary to realise that, due to its complex nature, tourism requires an analysis of sustainability broken down into multidimensional issues. Looking at the development of tourism must use environmental, social, economic, cultural, political and spatial prisms.

In academic circles, the prevailing idea is that, in order to be sustainable, development must ensure social equity, economic efficiency and environmental preservation in a balanced way. However, in the specific case of tourism and, even more so, ecotourism, the issues of social inclusion and environmental preservation must be emphasised before the question of economic efficiency.

In this way, according to Harvey (1992), analysing the contemporary moment from the point of view of the issues implicit in what can be called post-modernity, allows us to advance in the reflection of tourism not only from the point of view of an activity of financial capitalism, but in its interrelationship with the social, cultural and environmental phenomena of which it is an integral part and which, if on the one hand it affects them, as so many authors have analysed, it is also subjected to and affected by.

Qualifying a territory for the implementation of post-tourism requires reflection on the assessment of the impacts on nature caused by human and ecological flows, especially in areas of recent expansion. In the quest to qualify these territories, the identification of the elements of space, nature, culture and society are fundamental to the interdisciplinary analysis of the space used by man.

Unlike mass tourism, which predominated in the 1950s to 1970s, the new trend in tourism is alternative tourism, according to Krippendorf (2000), personalising the tourism product and meeting the expectations of tourists, who increasingly value meaningful personal experiences. Post-tourism therefore shares this trend of expressing oneself through rewarding experiences that make it possible to feel the culture that is being visited and to feel the characteristic peculiarities of the place.

Panosso Neto (2005) listed three phases of tourism studies, which various thinkers defend in specific terms: the Pre-Paradigmatic, which defines uniqueness, the first fixed thoughts, the Paradigmatic, which presents tourism as a large system, and the New Approaches, which is based on the second phase with a much more focussed approach to the human being.

But just as the author described above, tourism is coming up with New Approaches, or it can also be called Post-Tourism, with an increasing focus on social thinking, on issues that will benefit and privilege the users of the assets that make up tourist attractions, so that the generations in question and future ones can glimpse the privileges they have as a whole in the localities. This translates into a sustainable approach, seeking to protect and preserve what we have today in a way that perpetuates the regional potential that has been exploited commercially.

These are some of the reasons why cultural, ecological and naturalistic tourism have grown in people's preferences, and new post-modern identities will develop, especially in new demands created and materialised in different lifestyles and travel. In the world, it is estimated that 10% is the minimum quota for the protection of resources by the various nations, whether these units are grouped as integral protection units, whose basic objective is to preserve nature, or sustainable use units, where the aim is to make nature conservation compatible with the socio-environmental needs of the populations involved.

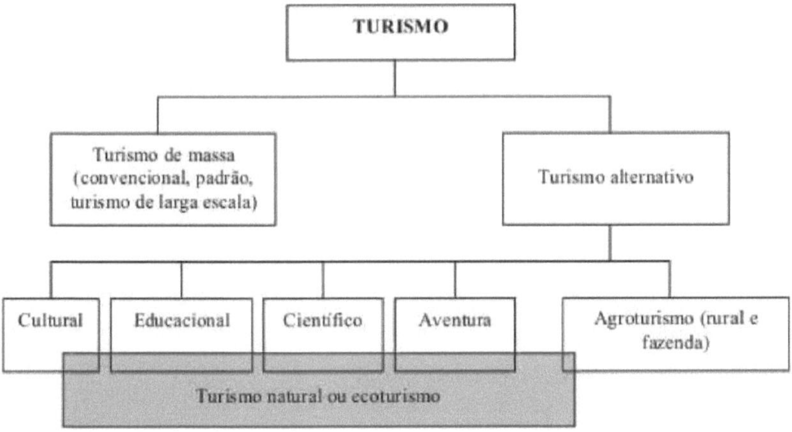

Illustration 04: Mass tourism and alternative tourism Source: Mieczkowsi (apud WEARING & NEIL, 2001, p.5)

Nature tourism or ecotourism, as presented above, seems to conceptually include all types of tourism that depend on the environment to be carried out, but differs from certain types of cultural tourism, carried out in museums and entertainment venues with artificial equipment.

The work in question sheds light on how ecotourism in protected areas is seen as an activity that can provide the monetary incentives needed to manage these areas. This activity generates minimal negative impact on the natural environment and produces few transformations or interferences in the way of life in the area visited. Currently, the idea of conserving natural resources as a means of generating economic resources through tourism is well received by communities.

In this way, alternative tourism is the antithesis of mass tourism in that it is concerned with limiting the tourist flow and is carried out on a small scale, unlike mass tourism, which is carried out on a large scale (KHAN, 2003). Alternative tourism or post-tourism retains another fundamental characteristic, which is respect for the place visited or sense of place (WEAVER, 1998).

Given this new trend, the UNWTO (2006) in its Travel and Tourism Barometer report projects that annual growth in Europe's tourist flow from 2020 onwards will be 4.6 per cent, compared to 3.3 per cent today. However, these statistics show that the eastern countries will have even higher rates: 8.5 per cent in the Russian Federation; 8.4 per cent in Croatia; 6.2 per cent in Slovenia; 5.5 per cent in Turkey and 5.2 per cent in Bulgaria. These regions can be labelled as reservoirs of curiosity, which explains their great power to attract post-modern tourist demand. In other words, we can infer that destinations with exotic cultures, unique landscapes and history little known to the media will be the niche tourist markets of the future.

It is also projected that in 2020, the world's main tourist destinations by tourist arrivals will be China first, followed by France, the USA, Spain and Hong Kong (CARVÃO, 2009). Another trend that has emerged in recent years, as mentioned above, is the development of emerging economies such as China, India and Russia. This has led to an increase in the middle class with purchasing power and disposable income to travel, initially within their own country, then within their own region and then to other regions. This trend has been particularly evident in Asian source markets (CARVÃO, 2009).

According to this overview, Van der Berghe's (1994) concept is in line with our thinking, as he argues that:

"independent tourists interact much more with locals and in more varied ways than guided tourists". In this way, it should be noted that a new, more conscious and ethical tourist profile is necessary for a more responsible tourist activity, since interaction that respects local cultures is fundamental.

It can be seen that the post-tourist is a consumer who is looking for diversified quality in the services provided by the destination visited, valuing culture in all its complexity and particularity, moving in search of icons that represent local identity and the collective memory represented by the tangible and intangible cultural goods that make up heritage.

These tourists are also aware that natural landscapes must be preserved, as they are part of an environment that will offer the populations involved a more qualitative survival, with good expectations for the growth of future generations that are part of this history. Therefore, the environmental and cultural formation of this new demand refers to a set of experiences, historical facts and common elements experienced by this different profile of consumers who are more responsible for the development of sustainable tourism.

As such, this profile of tourist is a person whose trust is not easily gained, and who no longer accepts packages pre-determined by travel agents, indicating what kind of attraction they should consume, since the traveller themselves wants to move between contrasts and discover new attractions to visit.

And as a way of emphasising this context, Talaya (2004) states that:

> there is a traditional profile of tourists, but with the passage of time and the various adaptations that have taken place, taking into account mainly scientific and technological innovations, new profiles of tourists will emerge, as well as greater segmentation of markets and tourist destinations.

The author states that the aspects that motivate travelling have changed. One example is the sun and beach destination, considered one of the traditional motivational options, which is now being replaced by various other types of destinations, with different characteristics, such as cultural tourism, ecotourism, rural tourism, among others. These changes in behaviour, which are also influenced by environmental issues, are altering the structure of market behaviour, which is trying to adapt by segmenting itself according to the diversity of the new demand.

Those who seek post-modern tourism are looking for a place that is different from what they normally live in, trying to find new emotions and new knowledge that can be contained in a new geographical identity that is not simply a new landscape: "the affirmation of the personality of the place, made up of multiple human identities and the natural world, is justified as significant references for everyday life (...) that make it possible to resist various aspects of globalisation" (YÁSIGI, 2001, p.44).

In this search for a differentiating factor, we can mention a particular feature for attracting visitors to new destinations: the exoticism of the place, which is becoming an increasingly valued characteristic in the tourism market. This is why Ribeiro (1999) describes this contemporary or post-modern tourist as an individual who needs to differentiate themselves through environmentalist ideologies, seeking to restructure their own identity.

Similarly, Sampaio (2000) infers that in order to attract these new tourists, the adoption of the precepts of sustainability in this model of tourist destination determines, first and foremost, an ideological change, from which lasting local development becomes the objective to be achieved, which does not mean the prevalence of one of the systems over the others, much less the abandonment of one of them, but it does include the aforementioned equity and balance in the development of the economic/sociocultural/environmental triad.

In defence of the economic viability of implementing sustainability principles, respect for the environment and socio-cultural issues, the UNWTO (2001) cites the growing demand from conscious tourists looking for well-preserved destinations (in every aspect) that can meet this requirement, including being willing to pay more for the product that meets their needs.

Updating this quote, we can add that at this year's World Economic Forum, a Tourism and Travel Competitiveness Report was drawn up, which attempted to measure the percentage of tourists seeking sustainable tourism and came up with a percentage that is believed to be around 6% of the total of around one billion tourists currently travelling the world. So we can see that it's a low figure, but with real possibilities of increasing due to the greater engagement of the entire tourist trade, governments, organisations and tourists who are beginning to understand that sustainability in tourism is the best way forward.

And in fact, in order to succeed in involving all those who make up tourism, it is necessary to enable planning as a process at the service of well-being and sustainability. According to Hall (2004), it is unquestionable that planning points towards the future, towards the construction of a desirable and sustainable scenario,

> [...] it can minimise potentially negative impacts, maximise economic returns to destinations and thus stimulate a more positive response from the host community towards tourism in the long term. (HALL, 2004, p. 29)

When analysed, it can be argued that tourists want to experience authentic activities in the places, events and festivals, no longer being supporting actors but becoming active in the local community. This means that tourist groups will become smaller and smaller, fostering intimacy between people who can change the programme through a climate of complicity.

As an illustration of this, according to data from the UNWTO (2001), in the document Tourism Vision 2020, it can be seen that the projections for Africa, East and South Asia, the Pacific and the Middle East will be growing in terms of the number of visitors with the profile of post-tourists, on the other hand, This leads us to believe that the prospects for the development of post-modern tourism are positive in regions that are privileged from the point of view of their natural and cultural heritage, but poor economically, which requires special care in the planning of these locations.

However, everything explained so far in this work will be invalid if the construction of a new tourism ethic is not consolidated and disseminated throughout society. When it comes to environmental ethics in tourism, the aim is to understand the different behavioural attitudes of all sectors of tourism towards nature, and in this line of ecological thinking Boff (2004, p.22) mentions that: "ethics would also be to potentiate generational solidarity in the sense of respecting the future of those who have not yet been born".

Today's society also needs to be mobilised to take on a more participatory role, capable of questioning, in a concrete way, the government's lack of initiative in implementing policies relating to sustainability and development, in a context of increasing difficulty in promoting social inclusion.

In this sense, environmental responsibility is linked to citizenship and both are favourable topics for debate, reflection and awareness-raising in order to act towards tackling socio-environmental problems.

We realise that the exercise of citizenship represents the possibility of opening up spaces for the implementation of different alternatives for participatory democracy, as it offers guaranteed access to information and the consolidation of different spaces and moments that encourage plural participation.

From this perspective, environmental ethics is an attempt to understand the relationship between human beings and the other elements of nature, and what values permeate the different relationships established. It is therefore understood that a moral education is needed to form free and autonomous individuals who are capable of living harmoniously in society, becoming an integral part of their environment and also transforming it in order to make it better for everyone, but also individuals who are capable of building more responsible relationships with the environment and other living beings, guided by values that allow them to collaborate in transforming the planet's degradation.

As you can see, the exercise of citizenship is a process under construction that involves political, cultural and social education, among others, because it should point to the exercise of socio-environmental justice in the relationship between man and nature and man and man, since it is everyone's right to live in a healthy environment, free from any damage that could jeopardise life.

Reflecting on the above vision, environmentally friendly tourism offers a model that is closer to the right one for the entire management of the tourist trade to work in compliance with environmental legislation, within the appropriate parameters of the limitations imposed by the natural environments of the places visited. Therefore, sustainable tourism is not about a tourism segment, but a model to be followed by all tourism sectors, contributing to the future development of a locality.

To summarise, as a way of understanding the importance of post-modern tourism, the concept of sustainable tourism can be brought to the fore, given by Ferreira (2004, p.74) who says:

> Sustainable tourism is tourism that meets the needs of the market, current tourists and host communities, utilising natural and cultural resources without compromising the ability of future generations to enjoy these same resources.

In other words, it's possible to understand post-tourism in a way.

modern tourism in the light of sustainable tourism, since the terminology of the term is not yet officialised by the UNWTO, but has been studied by various authors with certain divergences of concepts, however in this work, by reviewing the sources consulted, it was preferred to adopt a line of thought close to the premises of more ethical tourism with socio-environmental responsibility that is also defended by Van der Berghe who is one of the references on this subject.

CHAPTER 4

SUSTAINABLE TOURISM MANAGEMENT

As has been emphasised throughout the arguments and references of this work, the world scenario has been changing rapidly, and the methods for analysing and intervening in it have had to adapt and expand, producing increasingly permanent and global changes. Thus, planning and management in these scenarios also need to provide new answers to current problems and create new strategies to replace those that are no longer efficient and effective for organisations, systems, processes and destinations. Society demands new, faster, more applicable and more flexible responses.

Management and planning are complementary, interrelated and dependent on each other in terms of their effectiveness. The management of each planning process needs to be efficient enough to pursue the proposed objectives, and intrinsically flexible enough to keep up with changes in the internal and external environments. Planning, in turn, needs to be concerned with the management of each process, which must take place continuously and systemically.

The basis of this study is linked to the nature of planning and management as human actions and their new approaches from the most diverse areas of human knowledge. These new situations require some changes and the overcoming of obstacles, many of them historical. The first barrier is overcoming the dichotomy between planning and implementation, or more practically, between project and execution.

When it is understood that the action of planning continues in management, proposal and implementation are linked from their very essence, because one process without the other is simply innocuous. This understanding guarantees the application of these two human actions in a global and complex perspective of the real world, even when dealing with local problems. The interrelationship, complementarity and dependence between planning and management require efficiency throughout the process.

Planning therefore needs to be flexible enough to ensure that the management of each process takes place continuously and systemically, resulting in efficient and effective strategies socially, ecologically and economically. Ensuring the efficiency and effectiveness of each process is directly linked to continuous evaluation and reassessment, making adjustments possible and guaranteeing the continuity and flexibility of processes, which are indispensable in this scenario of strong uncertainty and change. In this context, territorial planning and management needs to be presented as a comprehensive and flexible process, strongly linked to a systemic vision from a continuous perspective of sustainability.

For better performance and efficiency in destination management, this development must be carried out with the help of good tourism planning, which if drawn up in a participatory way with the community will be more efficient and closer to the reality experienced in the locality under study. This in itself is interesting if it has the participation and support of the local government and those interested in some way in regional development, even if they benefit more than others socially.

According to the object in question, tourism territories, from a systemic viewpoint, must have planning and management processes that at the same time place themselves as part of the environment that disrupts the system, increasing the possibilities for learning and evolution, optimising the processes of creation and innovation. In this scenario of rapid and often radical change, it is also up to planning and management to enable the system to understand its own structure.

It is recommended that sustainable tourism management carry out actions with space as the central variable, linked to other variables such as politics, the economy, society, culture and the natural environment.

The cultural legacy of sustainability can be traced back to the beginning of the 19th century. However, it was in the 20th century, due to globalisation, that sustainable development became a focus of the development process of an increasingly integrated society concerned with economic development and the responsible use of the environment (SACHS, 1993).

Tourist destinations that develop strategic management models geared towards sustainability guarantee a better position in the market and an improvement in local standards of living with greater benefits for the culture of the region, and the environmental, social and economic issues of the locality in general (HALL, 2004).

The existence of projects focussing on this issue is true, but there is also a lack of proactive projects and research in various regions, and concern is growing about the environmental crisis of natural resources.

When discussing macro-trends, we are not performing an exercise in futurology. What we are doing is rationally analysing current events that could have important impacts on the future. The phenomenon of tourism is susceptible to various factors that are being defined in a globalised world, at the same time as it itself has caused more or less radical changes depending on the region under analysis. In the Caribbean, for example, the impact of tourism is intense, accounting for one in six jobs and an average of 50.0% to 70.0% of the GDP of the 30 countries in the region (NAISBITT, 1998).

In recent years, there has been an increase in favourable tourism statistics around the world and Brazil is no different, as it has shown good results in terms of national and international tourist flows, proving to be an activity with great potential for the country's economic development. Despite these results and the progress made with the National Tourism Policy, resulting from the decentralisation of the 2003/2007 National Tourism Plan, there are still limitations in terms of integration between the different spheres of government, between the public sector and the private sector, with repercussions on planning, coordination and evaluation of results.

We believe that the supporting role of tourism administration in this scenario needs to be changed, or rather, it needs to play a leading role in the various functions that add to the activity, helping to increase society's participation in the management process.

It is believed that the management proposal should function as a national planning system, where the participation and responsibility of each level of public and private administration is clear, with their respective partnerships. For this to happen, it is essential to define planning and management benchmarks for tourism at these various scales of action, such as plans and programmes, in an articulated manner.

In order to improve the tourism planning and management process, it is necessary to discuss what the main forces are and what their impact will be, which can be identified or categorised as facts that portend the future or strongly influence tourism. Based on studies by various trend analysts, including Goeldner, Ritchie and McIntosh; Porto, Nascimento and Buarque; and Naisbitt (2002; 2001; 1998), the following, among others, can be cited as potentially influencing the tourism sector:

1. Environmentalism and the challenge of sustainability;
2. Spread of democracy: increased pressure for community participation;
3. Demographic changes;
4. Diversity in a homogeneous world;
5. Technological revolution, the emergence of the virtual economy and the new knowledge society;
6. Reducing the power of nation states to intervene in tourism development;
7. The new colonialism and the increase in the number of people affected by social exclusion (differences between North/South nations);
8. The economic imperative and the instability of the global financial system;
9. The search for stability and security.

Agreeing with this idea and reinforcing the public role in the activity, Elliott (1997) argues that only governments are strong enough to guarantee the political stability, security and legal and financial structure that tourism requires. With the same focus, Ignarra (2002, p.125) considers that "it is not possible to produce tourism without the direct and indirect participation of public authorities", since government action plays a strategic role in its development.

Making a brief critical reference to mass tourism, the management of this activity continues to cater to groups of visitors who use the services of travel agencies or operators to organise their trip. These, in turn, are carried out without any customisation, prioritising visits to the main attractions in a short space of time, often less than that needed for proper enjoyment.

As a result of this type of tourist development, the main destinations in the states are overcrowded and the tourist experience they offer is negatively impacted by the excessive number of visitors and the profile of the visit, with stays in large hotels, overloaded visits to easily accessible attractions and little interaction with the places visited.

In this way, mass visitation is one of the most prominent characteristics of tourism on the north-east coast of Brazil today.

According to the Ministry of Tourism (BRASIL, 2005), sun and beach destinations attract tourists of average socio-economic status, whose stay is directly linked to the packages purchased from travel operators, and hardly ever exceeds five to seven days. These are visitors with planned expenses, who only visit the main attractions of the state's best-known destinations and do so with large groups of visitors, which can diminish the tourist experience.

However, the objectives of this study are to ensure that post-modern tourism can and should contribute to a more sustainable management of the activity. To this end, Beni (1991) mentions three important elements for the future management of tourism: innovation (creativity, imagination, questioning), performance (productivity) and quality (professionalism and the permanent search for customer satisfaction).

In addressing these elements, Beni (1991) translates the conceptual bases of post-tourism that are defended in this research, as it is believed that management for the rational development of tourism activity should be guided by these elements and by principles and practices that help achieve the desired development scenario, optimising the services provided. At this juncture, this information on post-modern tourism is aimed at the development and subsequent maintenance of tourist activity and aims to minimise the occurrence of environmental, economic or socially unsustainable practices.

At this point, by building on the knowledge obtained throughout this work, we can bring up some guidelines for the strategic management of post-tourism that can follow these lines:

- Preserving nature and maintaining biodiversity;
- Valuing the tangible and intangible cultural diversity of social groups;
- Encouraging the construction of equipment and physical structures that are economically viable and associated with the landscape (natural or urban) in which they are located;
- Encouraging the creation of tourism products aimed at different audiences, considering local, regional, national and international tourists;
- Support for the development of alternative niche markets to mass tourism;
- Encouraging the spatial expansion of the state's tourist destinations, with a view to internalisation and deconcentration of the activity on the coast;
- Expansion of job and income opportunities for the state's population;
- Investment in human resources as a way of developing tourism;

• Striving for quality in the provision of tourist services;

• Co-operation between the public, private and third sectors at municipal, regional, state and national level;

• Acting in accordance with the state's regulatory and legal frameworks, taking into account local and regional peculiarities.

To this end, these guidelines can be drawn up in an integrated and strategic way in a practical systemic framework for application in a given tourist destination as a model of sustainable governance, as shown in the diagram below:

SYSTEMS	SPECIFICITY	SIMILARITY	STRATEGIC COMPONENTS
Quality Management	- Organising processes - Process monitoring - Product monitoring	-Integrated policy -Documentation: integrated management manual, procedures, instructions and records	-Collectivist political management -Specialised commercial management -Long-term financial management
Environmental Management	- Analysing environmental aspects - Analysing environmental impacts - Compliance with environmental laws - Environmental Management Plan	-Internal audits - Corrective action - Preventive action	-Management of Resources Flexible and collectivist humans
Health and Safety Management	- Analysing health risks - Analysing security risks -Service to first aid rules -Emergency Public Use Plans	- Continuous improvement - Critical analysis by management and employees	- Production management of multipurpose -Sustainable tourism management

Illustration 05: Integrated Management System Model Source: NASCIMENTO (2016)

With all these coordinated guidelines, we hope to have a sustainable tourist destination, with efficient management that fosters a healthy city. The results are therefore: improved and personalised services offered by the receptive services to their visitors; a collective attitude that is favourable to tourism; a community attitude that is aware of the benefits that the activity is capable of providing, with the city being the tourist company itself; the appreciation of a material and immaterial cultural identity in all aspects of the municipality/region visited; the self-esteem of the local people will be marked and a commitment to market ethics will be prioritised throughout the tourism production chain.

We realise that the first step has already been taken, although it is still a slow process with many obstacles, as has already been discussed here, but we must move forward in all spheres of management and administration, focusing on the development and implementation of mechanisms for monitoring and evaluating the performance of tourism activity, whether in terms of the effectiveness of specific actions taken to achieve the proposed objectives and targets, or in terms of the effectiveness of the results for the development of tourism, with sustainability.

CHAPTER 5

METHODOLOGICAL PROCEDURES

This section presents the paths taken during the research, its design, scope, methods and techniques used. Nascimento (2007, p.23) says:

> Academic work aims to construct a thought and perpetuate ideas through it. To do this, it is necessary to seek out concepts and analyses from theorists and thinkers who are opinion formers and represent contemporary scientific knowledge.

Discussions about new ethical relationships between society and nature are recent, dating back to the second half of the 20th century. The inclusion of this theme in theoretical productions on sustainable tourism is also recent.

As already mentioned, "content analysis" as proposed by Bardin (2009) was used to analyse the full texts. According to this author, "content analysis" can currently be understood as:

> [...] A set of increasingly subtle methodological tools that are constantly being perfected and applied to extremely diverse "discourses" (contents and continents). The common factor of these multiple and multiplied techniques - from calculating frequencies that provide encrypted data to extracting structures that can be translated into models - is a controlled hermeneutic based on deduction: inference. As an effort at interpretation, content analysis oscillates between the two poles of rigour of objectivity and fecundity of subjectivity. It both absolves and cajoles the researcher by its attraction to the hidden, the latent, the unseen, the potential for the unseen (the unspoken), retained by any message. (BARDIN, 2009, p.11)

Thus, the references consulted to support the theme of mass tourism and environmental impacts were: Barretto (1995); Dantas (1999); Ruschmann (1997); OMT (2005, 2006);

Fennell (2002); Cooper et al. (2001), from which we can learn more about the conceptualisation and history of mass tourism, understanding its relationship with environmental impacts.

On the subject of post-modern tourism and environmental ethics, during the literature review we came into contact with important references in each area, such as: Harvey (1992); Krippendorf (2000), Van der Berghe (1994); Talaya (2004); Sampaio (2000); OMT (2001); Hall (2004); Boff (2004); Ferreira (2004). Therefore, with these citations throughout the work, it was possible to enrich the discussions and arguments that raised the importance of research and understanding the concept of sustainable management.

In order to make the data more reliable, it was decided to research statistical data from official sources related to the object of study and with recent records. In this way, projections of future scenarios can be drawn up in accordance with the objectives set out in the scope of the work.

As this is qualitative research, it is based on a humanistic vision that is concerned with a series of meanings that permeate social life (MINAYO, 1992). We found it necessary to carry out a document-based study, adopting Bardin's interpretative methodology, which aims to conceptualise and confront the key words of this research. In this way, we sought out authors with proven recognition in national and international literature in order to support the work in question.

CHAPTER 6

FINAL CONSIDERATIONS

In the same way that starting the study is a great challenge, concluding it is a difficult task, since this long investigative journey has been guided by debates, discussions, questions, research and reflections involving the phenomenon of tourism, the environment, management and sustainability, themes that are becoming increasingly important in today's society, so we believe we have helped to deepen these themes.

This research provides relevant support for a more in-depth study into development paths and sustainable strategies based on the multiple potentialities encompassed by post-modern tourism.

It may not be possible for current or even future generations of researchers to dimension and explain all the multidimensional complexity of the objective in question. The aim of this work is to contribute to elucidating the issue in order to provide theoretical support for a systemic analysis of sustainable tourism management.

However, many studies have linked environmental ethics to environmental education, giving the latter the role of developing this "new ethic". The appropriation by the field of Environmental Education of discussions on the ethical relationship between society and nature must therefore take place very carefully, since they will be reflected not only in the theoretical field but also in educational practices.

Faced with the major challenges facing civilisation at the beginning of the third millennium, the discussion about the direction to be taken in dealing with environmental issues is taking centre stage. Never before has the concern with the preservation of life on the planet, in its most varied forms, and with improving the means necessary to maintain the natural heritage been so much on the agenda, giving rise to greater involvement on the part of society in defining the principles that should govern its relationship with the environment that surrounds it.

This academic production was guided by the theoretical and methodological debates on the phenomenon of tourism, specifically by the approaches of mass tourism with its impacts and post-modern tourism with its new ideology. Within this logic, we sought to meet the objectives raised in this work; analysing the purpose of post-tourism; understanding how this activity can be sustainable; and identifying the challenges and prospects for promoting more rational management.

The future of tourism looks promising from an economic and social point of view. What remains to be seen is how to manage its impact on natural and cultural heritage and how to distribute the wealth generated more equitably, given that the trend, according to John Naisbitt, is for a huge increase in travel over the next few decades:

> As borders open, populations mature and become more prosperous, and governments, educators and the private sector continue to promote tourism as a basic human right, people will travel like never before (NAISBITT, 1998, p.151).

The general objective of the research was achieved by understanding how the model of post-modern tourism or post-tourism can be made viable for the implementation of sustainable management in the sector, since in order for it to become practicable it is necessary to engage the community, the private sector and the public sphere in its planning. In order to seek alternatives and opportunities for greater segmentation of the tourism market, thus fostering: alternative products, exotic attractions, personalised services, clean technologies, conscious consumers and multidisciplined professionals.

However, co-operation between all the sectors and actors that make up tourism is still in its infancy, making it extremely difficult for this proposal and new concept to be definitively introduced as a way of attracting visitors to a new tourism market.

It has emerged that governments need to be more involved, giving more importance to tourism in the local development of regions. New consumers of this activity with proactive thinking and behaviour have changed the way they act and use assets in a more conscious and sustainable way (SWARBROOKE and HORNER, 2002).

It is understood from the theory reviewed that post-tourism is nothing more than what is being practised in some segments, such as agro-tourism, ecotourism and others that have sustainable and substantial characteristics, which are: uniqueness, social interrelationship, valorisation of local culture, rationality of natural resources, creativity and the search for the exotic. With regard to the environmental approach, this work can elucidate that such a model tends to minimise the negative impacts of tourism on the environment, contributing to efficient and optimised management of environmental and tourist services in localities.

Thus, we can infer that the expected increase in the volume of tourists, with an increasingly dispersed distribution around the world, the change in the profile of visitors in tourism, with greater education and more awareness of their role in society and the development of new forms associated with nature and culture is essential to make the tourist activity more ethical. We therefore believe that more selective and demanding behaviour on the part of post-modern tourists will require consistent measures in tourism planning with a view to guaranteeing the sustainable development of the activity.

It was noted that the changeability of these elements, through economic, social and cultural factors, directly affects environmental and cultural heritage, as well as the lifestyle of the communities that become tourist destinations, and therefore requires constant reviews and improvements in planning, management and control processes.

The work presented here thus contributes to the analysis of tourism systems. It is suggested that it be used for case studies in mass tourism destinations, both in the areas of public administration focused on tourism development and those dedicated to contemporary urban activities with tourism potential. Furthermore, this object of study should be useful in the professional practice of tourism planners and managers, helping them to adopt appropriate strategies for cases of destinations that aim to be sustainable.

REFERENCES

1. ANDERECK, K. L. Envionmental consequences of tourism: a review of recent research. In: McCOOL, Stephen F. and WATSON, Alan. **Linking tourism, the environment, and sustainability**. Topical volume of compile papers form a special session of the annual meeting of the National Recreation and Park Association. Minneapolis, MN, 1994.

2. ANDRADE, J. **Turismo**: fundamentos e dimensões. São Paulo: Ática, 1992.

3. ANDREU, M. G. N. **Ecotourism, nature conservation and local development:** the cases of Mexico, Central America and the Greater Antilles. Doctoral thesis, Universitat Rovira I Virgili, 2003.

4. BARDIN, L. **Content analysis**. Revised and updated edition. Lisbon: Edições 70, 2009.

5. BARTHOLO JUNIOR, R.S. **The crisis of industrialism:** genealogy, risks and opportunities. In: BURZSZTYN, M., LEITÃO, P. & CHAIN, A. (eds.) Que crise é esta? São Paulo: Brasiliense, 1984.

6. BARRETTO, M. **Manual de iniciação ao estudo do turismo**. Campinas- SP: Papirus, 1995. 163 p.

7. BENI, M. C. **Product and service quality**. In: Tourism in Analysis. São Paulo. ECA/USP, 2, nov.1991, p.7-13.

8. BOFF, L. **Ecologia**: grito da guerra, gritos dos pobres. Rio de Janeiro: Sextante, 2004.

9. BUCKLEY R. Natural Area Tourism: Ecology, Impacts and Management. **Annals of tourism research**, Great Britain, Elsevier Science, Vol. 30, No. 2, p. 497-499, 2003.

10. BRAZIL. Ministry of Tourism. **Basic tourism statistics**, 2005. Available at < http://www.turismo.gov.br>. Accessed on 05 May 2009.

11. CARVÃO, S. **Trends in international tourism**. Madrid: Exedra, 2009. 32p. (Exedra - Tourism and Heritage).

12. CARVALHO, I. S. H. de. **Potentials and limitations of the sustainable use of biodiversity in the cerrado:** a case study of the grande sertão co-operative in northern Minas Gerais. Brasília: UNB, 2007.

13. CASTROGIOVANNI, A. C. In: Tourism X space: necessary reflections in postmodernity.In: CASTROGIOVANNI, A . C.; GASTAL, S. **Turismo na pós-modernidade**: (des)inquietações. Porto Alegre: EDIPUCRS, 2003, p. 43-50.

14. COOPER, C; FLETCHER, J; WANHILL, S; GILBERT, D; SHEPHERD, R. **Turismo**: princípios e prática. 2. ed. Porto Alegre: Bookman, 2001.

15. CORIOLANO, L.N.M.T. **Conceptual bases of development and ecotourism**. In Turismo e Ambiente: Temas Emergentes. Queiroz, O.T.M.M. São Paulo, 2006.

16. CRUZ, R. C. da. **Introduction to the geography of tourism**. São Paulo: Roca, 2001.

17. DANTAS, A. L. de F. L. **Tourist activity and sustainable paths: a case study in the municipality of Rancho Queimado - SC**. 1999. 95p. Dissertation (Master's

Degree in Production Engineering. Postgraduate Programme in Production Engineering) - Federal University of Santa Catarina, Florianópolis, 1999. Available at< http://teses.eps.ufsc.br/tese.asp>. Accessed on 29 April 2009.

18. DIAS, R. **Sustainable tourism and the environment**. São Paulo: Atlas, 2003.

19. EAGLES, P.F.J.; MCCOOL, S. F.; HAYNES, C.D.A. **Sustainable tourism in protected areas**: Guidelines for Planning and Management. Switzerland and Cambridge: IUCN Gland, 2002.

20. ELLIOTT, J. **Tourism**: politics and public sector management. London: Routledge, 1997.

21. FENNELL, D. A. **Ecotourism**: an introduction. São Paulo: Contexto, 2002.

22. FERREIRA, L. F. Capacity building for ecotourism and the involvement of host communities. In: LAGE. Beatriz Helena Gelas (eds). **Turismo, hotelaria e lazer**, 3 ed. São Paulo: Atlas, 2004.

23. GARROD, B. & FYALL, A. Beyond the rhetoric of Sustainable tourism? **Tourism management**, Great Britain: Elsevier Vol. 19, No 3, p. 199-212, 1998.

24. GOELDNER, R. C.; RITCHIE, J.R.B. & MCINTOSH, R.W. **Tourism:** Principles Practices and Philosophies. 8th Ed. Trad. Roberto Cataldo Costa. São Paulo: Bookman, 2002.

25. HALL, M. **Tourism planning**: policies, processes and relationships. São Paulo: Contexto Publishing House, 2004.

26. HARVEY, D. The **postmodern condition**: an enquiry into the origins of social change. São Paulo: Loyola, 1992.

27. IGNARRA, L. R. **Fundamentals of tourism**. São Paulo: Pioneira Thomson Learning, 2001.

28. KHAN, M. Ecoserv Ecotourist's: Quality Expectations. **Annals of tourism research**, Great Britain: Eselvier Science, Vol. 30, No. 1, 2003, pp. 109-124.

29. KRIPPENDORF, J. **Sociologia do turismo**: para uma nova compreensão do lazer e das viagens. São Paulo: Aleph, 2000.

30. LAGE, B. H. G.; MILONE, P. C. Global socio-economic impacts of tourism. In: LAGE, B. H. G.; MILONE, P. C. (org). **Tourism**: theory and practice. São Paulo: Atlas, 2000. ch. 11, p.117-131.

31. Leslie, D. **Responsible tourism:** concepts, theory and practice. Oxfordshire, UK: CAB International, 2002.

32. MIHALIC, T. Environmental management of a tourist destination A factor of tourism competitiveness. **Tourism management**, Great Britain, 2, 2000, pp.65-78.

33. MINAYO, M.C.S. **O desafio do conhecimento**: pesquisa qualitativa em saúde. São Paulo-Rio de Janeiro: Hucitec-Abrasco, 1992.

34. NAISBITT, J. **Global paradox:** the bigger the world economy, the more powerful its minor players. Trad. Ivo Korytovski. 2nd ed. Rio de Janeiro: Campus, 1998.

35. NASCIMENTO, H. H. O. **Identity, memory and conservation**: an analysis of tourism and cultural heritage in Touros/RN. 2007. 81p. Monograph (Bachelor's Degree in Tourism) - Federal University of Rio Grande do Norte, Natal, 2007.

36. UNWTO - World Tourism Organisation. **WTO world tourism barometer,**

Vol. 4, 2006. Available at:<http://www.worldtourism.org/facts/wtb.html>. Accessed on 2nd May 2009.

1.1. **Introduction to research methodology in tourism**. São Paulo: Roca, 2005.

1.2. **Introduction to tourism**. São Paulo, ed. Roca, 2001.

1.3. **Tourism 2020 vision**, 2001. Available at: < http://www.world-tourism.org/facts/wtb.html>. Accessed on 19 July 2009.

1.4. **Tourism highlights**, 2005 edition. WTO: Madrid, 2005. Available at:< http://www.world-tourism.org/facts/wtb.html>. Accessed on 07 May 2009.

41. PANOSSO NETTO, A. **Filosofia epistemologia**. São Paulo: Aleph, 2005.

42. PORTO, C.; NASCIMENTO, E. P.; BUARQUE, S. C. **Cinco cenários para o Brasil 2001-2003**. Rio de Janeiro: Nórdica, 2001.

43. RIBEIRO, G. L. **Latin America and the development debate**. Indian Journal of Social Science Vol. III, no. 2: 271-295. 1990. Available at:< http://www.esocialsciences.com/home/index.asp>. Accessed on 10 May 2009.

44. RODRIGUES, A.B. Ecotourism - the limits of eco and ethics. In: Adyr Balastreri Rodrigues (org). **Ecotourism in Brazil** - possibilities and limits. São Paulo: Contexto, 2003.

45. RUSCHMANN, D. **Turismo e planejamento sustentável**. Campinas: Papirus, 1997.

46. SACHS, I. **Transition Strategies for the 21st Century**: Development and the

Environment. São Paulo: Studio Nobel, 1993.

47. SAMPAIO, C. A. C. **Strategic organisational management for sustainable development**: an alternative methodology for sustainable tourism planning. Tourism: Vision and Action. Itajaí, Vol. 3, no 6, p.97-115, Apr/Sep, 2000.

48. SMITH, A. **The Wealth of Nations:** Enquiry into its Nature and Causes. 2.ed. São Paulo: Nova Cultural, 1985.

49. SMITH, M. D.; KRANNICH, R. S. Tourism Dependence and Resident Attitudes. **Annals of tourism research**, Great Britain: Elsevier Science, Vol. 25, No 4, 1998, p.783- 802.

50. SWARBROOKE, J.; HONER, S. **Consumer behaviour in tourism**. São Paulo: Aleph, 2002.

51. TALAYA, E. A. **La naturaleza en el comportamiento del consumidor turístico**. In: IX Congresso AECIT - El uso turístico de los espacios naturales, S.l.: s.n, 2004. Available at: <http://www.aecit.org/publicaciones/publicaciones.htm>. Accessed on 15 July 2009.

52. URRY, J. **O olhar do turista** - lazer e viagens nas sociedades contemporâneas. 2a. ed. São Paulo: SESC/Studio Nobel, 1996.

53. VAN DER BERGHE, P. **The quest for the order**: ethnic tourism in San Cristóbal, México. Seattle/London: University of Washington Press, 1994. Available at:<http://lap.sagepub.com/cgi/content/abstract/35/3/87>. Accessed on 10 May 2009.

54. WAINBERG, J. Notes for a theory of tourism: the industry of difference. In: GASTAL, S. (org) **Turismo**: nove propostas para um saber- fazer. Porto Alegre, Ed.

dos Autores, 1998, p. 42-64.

55. WEAVER, D. B. **Ecotourism as mass tourism:** Contradiction or Reality? What's the difference between ecotourism and mass tourism? Not much, perhaps. Hotel And Restaurant Administration, Cornell University: Tourism - Cornell: Quarterly, April. 2001.

MIX
Papier aus verantwortungsvollen Quellen
Paper from responsible sources
FSC® C105338

Printed by Books on Demand GmbH, Norderstedt / Germany